How to Survive School

Illustrated by Jane Eccles

MACMILLAN CHILDREN'S BOOKS

To Paula, who knows all about how to survive school

First published 2006 by Macmillan Children's Books
a division of Macmillan Publishers Limited
20 New Wharf Road, London N1 9RR
Basingstoke and Oxford
www.panmacmillan.com

Associated companies throughout the world

ISBN-13: 978-0-330-43951-0
ISBN-10: 0-330-43951-0

1 3 5 7 9 8 6 4 2

A CIP catalogue record for this book is available from
the British Library.

Typeset by Tony Fleetwood
Printed and bound in Great Britain by Mackays of Chatham plc, Kent

Contents

Read This Book

If your teacher makes you jumpy
And the dinner lady's grumpy
You're feeling fraught and frumpy
Not to mention downright dumpy
Read this book!

If your schoolwork gets you freaky
Makes your nerves a little tweaky
When you need to be quite geeky
But your voice has gone all squeaky
With answers kind of creaky
Read this book!

If your road of life is bumpy
And the homework makes you humpy
All your custard has gone lumpy
So all your days are slumpy
You might crack like Humpty-Dumpty
Read this book!

David Harmer

School Records

Instructions to ensure that anything
connected with tedious, boring school
never bothers you again:

Become a computer wizard. (This may involve
attending school for a while to study IT.)

Break into school during the night. (Learn
science first, so you can disable alarms
and CCTV cameras. Eat school dinners to ensure
you've ingested enough carrots
to let you see in the dark.)

Find your way to the secretary's office.
(The geography you learned in school
will help you decipher the ground plan.)

Boot up the computer and type in the school's name.
(You will know how to do this
because you learned to spell in school.)

Speed is important. Try out every possible
combination of letters to find the password.
Make your fingers dance. (School PE lessons
will have made you agile.)

Locate your records and identify your name.
Press ENTER (which you will recognize
from learning to read in school).

Remove any negative comments about conduct,
missed homework and unexplained absences.
If WEAK appears in the text, substitute WONDERFUL.
(IT again.)

Switch off the computer and leave the premises,
reminding yourself that school
is a complete waste of time.

Alison Chisholm

Monday Vikram, Tuesday Dan

Be a master of disguise –
Be, each day, a different size,
Some days small and some days big –
Wear, each day, a different wig.

Use, each day, a different voice,
Change your name – there's so much choice!
Monday Vikram, Tuesday Dan –
Wednesday Rachel, Thursday Ann.

Monday   Tuesday   Wednesday   Thursday   Friday

Daily change your class or school
And it's better, as a rule,
If you, daily, change the mates
You hang out with by the gates.

If you're expert at this game
You will never get the blame —
For, no matter what you do . . .
How can blame be pinned on you?

Philip Waddell

7

S.O.S.

4 p.m.,
School playground,
Path blocked by bully.
I shrink,
Begin to panic . . .

And then it happens.

Bells ring! Orchestras play!
My knees are suddenly made of sterner stuff,
My scalp tingles with life.
I am transported through the mind-tunnel,
To the land of Save-Our-Skin.

My teeth are silver skewers – Gnash!
My head twizzles on its stalk and snakes writhe from my
    skull – Hiss!

I hold my flaming lance aloft,
And my trusty steed champs at the bit.
Together we advance to meet the foe,
Who, overcome by my startling display of confidence,
Sneezes,
And is reduced to a very small pimple.

Mary Green

O Beautiful Cold Germs Today

O beautiful cold germs today
Are keeping me in bed.
I've got a tough math test to take,
Now I'll rest up instead.
O temperature, O temperature,
You've reached one hundred and three,
And now I get to lounge around
And play my new CD.

O runny nose all red with sneeze –
Some tissues by my side,
While all my classmates groan and sweat,
I'll view the TV guide.
O chicken soup, O chicken soup,
My mom will make for me,
And later I'll read comic books
And play Monopoly.

O little itty, bitty germs,
Although you make me mope,
You'll stay around a day or two
And then you'll leave, I hope –
For Saturday is coming soon,
Then I'll play with my friends
And really should be feeling good –
That's when my bed rest ends!

Robert Scotellaro

Pocket Time Machine

My pencil case is a time machine
It helps me to survive school.

If I haven't done my homework
I go back and do it.

If I do something wrong and the teacher sees
I go back and do it properly.

If I get done for being cheeky
I go back and say something really nice and supportive.

If I want to pass my tests
I go forward and find the answers (and sell them to my
    friends).

If I want to find out exactly what happened in 1066,
World War 2, to Winston Churchill or the Ancient Greeks
Easy peasy.

If I want to see what's going to be a great invention in
    2077
Or if England will win the World Cup again
    I can.

If I want to find embarrassing secrets about our
    teachers' past
Or what will happen to them in the future . . .
Guess what? Anything is possible.

I can go forwards and backwards
If I want – and when I want.

My pencil case is a time machine
It helps me to survive school.

See, I've gone back to the first line.

In fact I started this poem yesterday
And finished it tomorrow.

I might edit and rework it a hundred years ago
But methinks I shall not.

My pencil case is a time machine
It helps me to survive school.

Do you want to buy it?
I'll sell it to you tomorrow.

Paul Cookson

Escaping School

I crawl and creep across the field
It's raining and it's muddy
The teachers won't spot me at all
I'm hidden in my hoodie.

Smigsy tried it yesterday
He'd built a glider, had no doubts
The dinner ladies shot him down
With spud guns and three tonnes of sprouts.

Crystal tried to jump the fence
Like a bullet from a gun
The lollipop lady whacked her back
With her sign, it wasn't fun.

Jake and Jenny had a go
At leaping on a passing train
The Head got them with his lasso
They won't try that again.

A searchlight swings across the grass
I freeze beneath its glare
Hold my breath but it's all right
And now I'm nearly there.

Whoopee, I'm free, I've cut the fence
Wriggled though the hole
Oh no! Here comes the caretaker
With his Alsatian on patrol.

OK they've got me fair and square
I bow my head in sorrow
But then I smile cos they don't know
My tunnel starts tomorrow!

David Harmer

The Expert

Little Joe Horner
Sits in the corner
As quiet as a packet of peas
He wouldn't say boo
To a bucket of glue
And he always says thank you and please

He can't kick a ball
And he's no fun at all
In the playground he sits on his own
His writing is neat
And his homework's complete
Cos he always takes lots of work home

But he's the most popular
Boy in the class
Now you might think that odd, I agree
But he's expert at maths
And at science he's brill
And the best bit – he sits next to me

He'll give you a hand
If you're stuck with your sums
There is nothing that he doesn't know
If you can't add or measure
He'll help you with pleasure
And his charges are reasonably low

Roger Stevens

How to Survive School

(When your mum is Class 4's teacher and you are nine years old)

Wear a wig, dark glasses and a baseball cap at all times.

Be very very cheeky, take the fall
get sent to the head teacher's office
    for the rest of the day
working in total isolation on your own.

Play practical jokes first before they are done to you
and invent the best one ever
to be played on a Class 4 teacher.

Become nocturnal.
Demand to be fostered.

Conveniently lose your name badge
and every other named thing you own
including PE bag, book bag, pencil case, lunch box
(eat lunch first!) and rip/cut/bite out
the name labels from all your clothes.

If all else fails only answer to Elastigirl
and bend, stretch, pull yourself all ways
to dodge her.

Lesley Marshall

How to Drive Your Teacher Potty . . .

'If you've got ten pounds in one pocket,
And eight pounds in the other,
What have you got?' the maths teacher asked.
'The wrong trousers,' said little Sam Smother.

They were reading about Red Indians.
The teacher looked at her class,
'Now who was Hiawatha?'
She confidently asked.
They just sat there in silence,
They shrugged at one another,
Till Danny Dipstick said, 'Please, Miss –
Lowerwatha's older brother.'

The teacher asked Blodwyn, 'Where are you from?'
'Wales,' Blodwyn said, full of pride.
'Oh? Which part?' the teacher asked.
'All of me,' Blodwyn replied.

'Find Australia on the map,'
The teacher told Will White.
'It's there, Miss,' pointed Will at once.
The teacher said, 'That's right.'
And then she looked at Gormless Gus,

And said, 'Now tell me this,
Who discovered Australia?'
And Gus said, 'Will did, Miss.'

'Where's your homework?' teacher asked,
'It's missing yet again!'
'I did it, Sir,' the lad replied,
'But it's still inside my pen . . .'

Clive Webster

Sixteen Strategies for Surviving Silent Reading

Write a letter to your mum,
See how many times you can clench your bum.

Add up the number of words on a page,
Try to work out your teacher's age.

Practise telepathy with a mate,
Make a list of the things you hate.

Pull the funniest face you can,
Fold your bookmark into a fan.

Imagine yourself as a grizzly bear,
Have a go at eating your hair.

Think of the funniest joke you know,
Attempt to wiggle your little toe.

Count the hairs in your teacher's nose,
Close your eyes and take a doze.

Frighten your friends with your scariest look,
Oh, and you can always read a book!

Melissa Lawrence

Escape

A sunny afternoon is best
with the teacher in front
   talking . . .
     talking . . .
      talking . . .

You stare hard at the teacher
  – not too hard –
    about 80% concentration

At the same time
move your eyes just a little
  – not too much –
    towards your nose

Keep staring.

Slowly the teacher's outline
will sharpen at the edges
  – almost glow –
    and at the same time

become smaller . . .
    smaller . . .
        smaller . . .
as if viewed from the wrong end
of a telescope.

The voice will still be clear
but the words indistinguishable

and you are free to float
  dreaming . . .
    dreaming . . .
      dreaming . . .

Patricia Leighton

Nothing To Do With The Maths Test . . .

I know –
tomorrow I'll wake up with spots
and one tooth,
and eyebrows the colour of sick
and a limp
and folded-in ears
and various ankles
and a slight headache
and fish breath
and a twitch
and fungus fingernails

unable to remember . . . erm . . . ?
and rapid blinking
and an extra nostril
talking backwards
and the doctor will say
how brave I am
what with my worrying condition
and then he'll take me
to his friend the welder,
who'll make
a permanent exhibit
of my cast-iron excuse.

Stewart Henderson

Three All-Purpose Excuses

1. I've been very busy giving advice to the Prime Minister
   (this child is too important to argue with)

2. I spend most of my time living in a tent on Jupiter
   (this child is too ridiculous to know how to deal with)

3. In one of my former lives I was a tiger
   (this child is slightly weird, and may be dangerous)

Matt Black

Confused Homework Excuses

I couldn't do my homework because:
My baby brother made it into a cosy bed.
The doctor scribbled on it with a wax crayon.
A seagull said I was allergic to work at home.
Dad swooped down and carried it off.
My little sister lit a bonfire and burnt it.
Our parrot dropped it in the fish tank.
My dog said I didn't have to do it.

Mum slobbered all over it.
Aliens washed it in the washing machine with my
    trousers.
I took it into their spaceship thinking it was valuable.
My hamster forgot to take it home.

Chris Ogden

Strange Encounter

This is not Davy Haddon speaking.
Do not be alarmed, Davy is safe.

We have borrowed his body to walk through your world.
His mum and dad are safe.

Davy's sister is safe
(unless she reveals our secrets).

We have travelled through time and space
to learn more of your species.

You are the one they call 'teacher'.
We have learned from Davy of your kindness.

Please take this gobstopper as a gift.
We have come with a message,

a message that may be important in
the days to come.

The message is,
Davy will bring his homework in on Friday.

Hugh Waterhouse

How to Hide at School

I know the secret hidey holes
The places no one ever goes
Caretakers, cleaners, no one knows
Why I can hide at school

The cupboards and the corridors
The spaces underneath the floors
The places in and out of doors
How I can hide at school

Up above the ceiling tiles
Behind the teachers' unmarked files
Underneath recycling piles
Where I can hide at school

Down inside the staging blocks
Storerooms where I pick the locks
In the lost property box
When I hide at school

In the curtains in the hall
Just behind the toilet wall
I cannot let you know of all
The ways to hide at school

Practised them since I was five
Places I can hide and skive
It's the way you can survive
I've survived at school

Paul Cookson

Porridge

There is a place called No-thoughts,
where I sometimes go,
it's quite a nice place really
when I'm tired and slow.

It's a bit like a cabbage,
or porridge or a jelly,
or the inside of a marshmallow
or a switched-off telly.

It's like a hot summer classroom
where everyone is sleepy,
and No-ideas flop around on desks,
doing nothing, dreamy.

In this little place called No-thoughts
the teacher comes and goes,
and No-questions sink in slowly,
and no one answers, no one knows.

It's a bit like a cabbage,
or porridge or a jelly,
or the inside of a marshmallow
or a switched-off telly.

There is a place called No-thoughts,
where the flowers of No-thinking grow,
it's quite a nice place really
as No-thought places go.

Matt Black

A Note from Home

(Written by Lee, Who More Than Anything Else,
Was Afraid He May Have Spelt the Word 'MOM'
Backwards)

Deer Teechur,

Pleeze Ekcuze my good sun Lee
Heeze got the growscist alergee.
Eech time he takes a speling test
It gives him sorze akross his chest.
The speling kwizz will klog hiz noze
And give him boyills on hiz toze.
Hiz riting hand will swel and twittch
As all hiz porze beegin to ittch.
So just to make shure heeze ok
He shoodent take the test tooday.

Hiz MOM

Robert Scotellaro

The Six Worst Excuses in the World

1. The dog ate it.

mmm, English!

2. Someone left the window open, and a freak hurricane blew my book on the floor, and the dog ate it.

3. I put it in the hall, and a burglar broke into our house and stole it, and our next-door neighbour (who is a gorilla) rugby-tackled him on the lawn, and he dropped my book, and the dog ate it.

4. I'd just finished it when an extinct volcano at the end of our road suddenly erupted for the first time in ten million years and set fire to my book, and the firemen came and soaked it with their hoses, and as soon as it was dry the dog ate it.

5. I'd only left it for two minutes while I built a scale model of Buckingham Palace out of cheese triangles, when a whole herd of wildebeest stampeded through our back garden, battered down the kitchen door, and before they vanished into the shimmering sunset, they trampled my book under their mighty, thundering hoofs, and the dog ate it.

6. Here is a big box of your favourite chocolates instead. (Actually, THAT one works rather well.)

Clare Bevan

A Pupil's Prayer

Let me get in awful trouble,
let my school shoes grow too tight.
Let my bubbly not blow bubbles,
but,
let my sums be right.

May my birthday be forgotten,
may it rain all weekend long.
May I fall and bruise my bottom,
but please,
may my spellings not be wrong.

Let me lose my brand-new pencil case,
let my felt-tips all get nicked.
Let aunties kiss me all over my face,
but please, please,
let my tables all be ticked.

May there be no chocolate-chip ice cream,
may fleas invade my vest.
May I not get chosen for the team,
but please, please, please,
may I survive this rotten test.

David Horner

Helping Hand

There's a MAGIC WORD
That gets my school homework
Finished for me
When I haven't a clue
What to do
Or when I want to see
What's on TV
Or when I'm feeling bored
Or it's time for bed
Or I want to use
My computer instead.

'DA – A – AD!'

He just loves doing my homework
And getting it right –
So I shout my MAGIC WORD
Every night.

'DA – A – AD!'

'What is it, son?'

'I've got some more HOMEWORK
For you . . . !'

'Wow! THANKS!
How did I do last time . . . ?'

Trevor Harvey

My Best Subject

I'm no good at history, rubbish at maths
And geography, and all the rest;
But at blackmailing teachers I'm really quite good,
So I always do well in the tests.

Rob Falconer

Proposal at the School Council

In the playground
(Overnight)
I'd like to put
A few things right.
In one corner
I would make
A burger bar
For morning break.
Then by the bins
(Made spotless, clean)
I'd make a great big
Cinema screen.

Next to the wall
With the water fountain,
I'd pile up cushions
Like a mountain.
Then I'd cleverly
Rig the clock
So that, at playtime,
Time would stop.
Of course, for winter,
I'd fit a roof –
Retractable
And waterproof.
I hope you think
These alterations
Won't cause too much
Altercation!

Coral Rumble

Death by Worksheet

Our teacher's worksheet barmy
our school is worksheet mad.
She makes the biggest worksheets
the world has ever had.
We fill in all her questions
numbers, words and dates
adjectives and clauses
(copied from my mates).
>She says they 'test our knowledge'
>they tell her what we know
>who is quick and clever
>and who is very slow . . .
>>They tell her who remembers
>>parts of plants and names
>>wires and magnetism
>>>kings
>>>>and queens
>>>>>and reigns.

But I cannot remember
for I am rather slow
>as I gaze beyond the windows
>and dream of things I know.

Peter Dixon

Where to Sit on the Coach

When off on a school trip
here's a tip or two
from one who knows

Don't sit on the back seat.
You're bound to be spotted
waving out the window
and Darren will be making rude signs
at police cars
and you'll be caught up in the fun
and then you'll have to explain

to the police,
and the Head, when you get back,
and to your parents . . .
It's not worth it!

Don't sit at the front.
You'll have to talk to Mr Pleats
all the way there
about his collection of fossils
and then he'll start asking you
your eight times table.
And also
that's where they keep the sick bucket.

Sit about two-thirds back
if possible next to Cathy
the quiet girl with the hand-knitted socks
then you won't have to talk
and you can read your book
or listen to music
on your dad's iPod
which you borrowed this morning
or play games on your phone
which you smuggled on board
in your lunch box.

Roger Stevens

Ten Ways to Get Through Your Reading Book

(1) Change the hero's name to_____.

(2)   Start at the end.

(3) Read it under a micrOScope.

(4)   Read it from the far end of the room.

(5) ˙uʍop ǝpᴉsdn ʇᴉ pɐǝᴚ

(6) .sdrawkcab ti daeR

(7) Read it through dark glasses.

(8) Read it through one eye.

(9) Change the story by putting 'didn't' before every verb.

(10) Change every fifth word to_____.

Kate Williams

The Secret School Alarm

Somewhere in every school
Is a secret alarm.

Not the fire alarm
That's bright red and serious.

Not the burglar alarm
That's stuck on a wall.

This is a very special alarm
Tucked away and very tiny.

It's the I've-Had-Enough-Of-This-Place-
Do-Something-Quick Alarm.

Once you find it, smash the glass box
Press the bright blue buzzer.

A gigantic crack will open up in the yard
And swallow the Head and all the teachers.

It'll gobble up the bossy dinner ladies
And chomp down the dreaded school bullies.

Watch a fleet of ice-cream vans flood the playground
Full of free lollies, crisps and pop.

A circus full of clowns will take over the school
And start a massive custard-pie fight.

The whole place will go crazy for at least a week
No lessons at all and homework abolished.

Start searching today in the head teacher's office
Have a look around, under their desk,

Behind the curtain or the filing cabinet
Check the shelves and lift up the carpet.

Then it'll all kick off just like I said.
Honest.

David Harmer

John Turner's School Survival Manual

In class,
Adopt an angelic expression
At all times.
Memorize the following phrases:
Of course, Miss,
I'd love to, Miss,
That's no trouble at all, Miss.
(Or *Sir* depending on who your teacher is.
You need to be able to recognize
Which teachers are men
And which are women . . .)

Also –

If you're a girl,
Fiddle with your hair
And simper.

If you're a boy,
Put on your widest
And most pleasant smile.

If the teacher
Asks you a hard question,
Look enthusiastic and say –
Could I have just a couple of minutes more
To think about that, please . . .

If the teacher
Gives you homework, say –
I'm sure my mum will be pleased
To help me with this.
She's Chair of School Governors, you know.

In the playground,
Remind everybody of your
Older and tougher brother
Who's in Year 6
And who only narrowly escaped
Exclusion from school

Last autumn,
Following a certain
Unpleasant,
After-school incident . . .

Help your friends out
With their schoolwork
(But make sure that you're not *too* good at this —
You don't want them to think you're a Boff . . .)

Invite school friends for sleepovers
At your home.

Choose the ones with
The biggest houses
And the best PlayStation games.
With luck,
They'll invite you back . . .

When your parents ask you
How school is going, say —
Oh — fine — OK, you know.

(What do *they* know anyhow?
No way
They'd be able to survive
A single day in your school . . .)

Avoid sports day

And school dinners.

Always be polite

To the caretaker.

Pull your smile tight and

Enjoy every day . . .

John Turner

School Survival Kit

Pack the following every day:

1. Friendship
   (Friends make everything great)

2. A big smile
   (Who can resist that?)

3. A head full of jokes
   (To make others laugh)

4. A dollop of curiosity
   (To keep lessons interesting)

5. A packet of daydreams
   (For when they're not)

6. An ounce of courage
   (To face your fears)

7. A full battery of energy
   (To make playtimes fun)

8. A taste of adventure
   (To enjoy school trips)

9. A little understanding
   (So you can forgive those who let you down)

10. A bag full of joy
    (To share)

Karen Costello-McFeat

How to Survive Sports Day

On sports days I'm fast,
I'm always in the lead,
I'm the quickest in our class
as I gather speed.

I put out the beanbags
in no time at all,
and roll out the hoops
from inside the hall.

I set up the high jump
in less than a tick
and, in marking the pitch,
I know every trick.

I measure and check
without any delay,
for I'm really the star
of every sports day.

But it all goes wrong
when the races begin,
this is the moment
when I cannot win.

For at putting things out
I may be the best,
but at running I'm hopeless –
as you've probably guessed!

Andrew Collett

Survival Strategy

Finding it hard, surviving school?
Believe me, you're not unique!
So here's a slice
Of good advice
To get you through the week.

On misery Monday morning
Don't give in to glums and gloom.
Amid the grind
Just fix your mind
On Friday afternoon.

Tuesday's a well-known blues day:
Double maths is double doom.
Confused? Can't cope?

Then pin your hopes
On Friday afternoon.

Wednesday's worst is music:
'You're completely out of tune!'
Ignore derision,
Cling to your vision
Of Friday afternoon.

Thursday, that's school sports day:
You're last in the egg-and-spoon.
Enough of sports,
Direct your thoughts
Towards Friday afternoon.

Friday morning: nearly made it –
It'll all be over soon.
Take care, don't skive,
Arrive alive
At Friday afternoon.

You've cracked it then: your heart
Is light as a balloon.
It's half past three,
You're free! You're free!
On Friday afternoon.

Eric Finney

The Extreme Schools Survival Kit

Global Education Technology Inc. of Texas
Is proud to announce
The very latest Extreme Schools Survival Kit.

This year's model features the following exciting new
features:

The electronic 'teacher speak' translation tool,
To help you blag your way out of any tricky situation.
Simply type in your problem and the translator
Will turn it into an excuse no teacher can resist.

The HazChem uniform in your own school colours
That will keep you looking really cool
Even in those science lessons that go with a bang.

The microcomputer that slips over your thumbnail.
Indispensable, undetectable and always at your fingertips.
No need for maths to drive you mental any more.

The dictionary earpiece
That'll whisper sweet somethings in your ear.
Vital when you're lost for words in English,
Or next time you have that spelling test you forgot about.

The contact-lens globe
That'll help amaze your geography teacher.
Fit it snugly over one eye, blink,
And you can click on any feature anywhere in the world.

Last but not least,
The time-traveller watch that looks like
An ordinary timepiece on your wrist.
But set the digital display
And you can watch any period in
    history you choose.

We're so confident you'll want to invest
In our state of the art, high-tech kit
We're offering a complete money-back
    guarantee,
If not fully satisfied.

The Extreme Schools Survival Kit:
It's the ultimate school dress code.

From Global Education Technology Inc. of Texas.
G.E.T. I.T.!

Michael Lockwood

Tunnel Vision

We've started a tunnel,
Behind Dutton's desk,
To escape from next
Monday's PE.

O'Reilly is down there,
Digging away,
Then it's Mog,
Then Prejilla,
Then me.

If we do it well,
When 'Muscles' Morgan
Turns up, all
He'll see is a big,
Empty gym.

Deep underground,
He might just hear
The sound of us
Laughing and giggling at him.

I've planned that
Our tunnel ends
Over the road,
Somewhere cool . . .
Where do you think?

Five metres inside
Khan's Corner Shop,
Right next to the
Chocolate and drinks!

Mike Johnson

Count Down

193,536,848

193,536,845

193,536,842

193,536,839

193,536,836

193,536,833

193,536,830

193,536,827

193,536,824

193,536,821

193,536,818

193,536,815

193,536,812

193,536,809

193,536,806

193,536,803

193,536,800

193,536,797

193,536,794

193,536,791

193,536,788

193,536,785

193,536,782

193,536,779

193,536,776

193,536,773

193,536,770

193,536,767

193,536,764

193,536,761

193,536,758

193,536,755

193,536,752

193,536,749

193,536,746

193,536,743

193,536,740

193,536,737

193,536,734

193,536,731

193,536,728

193,536,725

193,536,722

193,536,719

193,536,716

193,536,713

193,536,710

193,536,707

193,536,704

193,536,701

193,536,698

seconds

till I leave

school forever

Nicholas Oram

How To Brazen Out Even The Toughest Interrogation From Any Teacher Even Though You Are 100% Guilty Of Everything They Are Accusing You Of!

Teacher: Why did you hit Jason?

You: Liam told me to do it!

Teacher: If Liam told you to jump off a cliff would you do it?

You: If I was going to land on Jason, yes.

Teacher: Go and stand on the wall!

You: OK.

Ian Bland

Education In

Education

in excuses:

sick as sawdust;

juicy mucous;

torpid tonsils;

spots exploding;

tongue in

plaster;

bones eroding;

<u>CUSES</u>

fatal fever;

head trans-

swollen

colon; mortal

planted;

colic; diarrhoea

brain decaying.

— diabolic;

Absence granted.

Gina Douthwaite

Why are we hiding in here?

Why are we hiding in here?
Why are we hiding in here?
What monsters are coming, what men in black?
What grim-clad figures on the attack?
Why are we hiding in here?

Why are we hiding in here?
Tell me the truth now, please.
Is it the taxman?
Is it the axeman?
Is it the secret police?

Why are we hiding in here?
Give me an answer, please.
Is it a giant slug?
Is it a superbug?
Is it that runny cheese?

There is nothing at all to fear,
Nothing at all to fear.
It's just the teacher with the funny grin.
If we keep really quiet he won't know we're in here!
That's why we're hiding in here . . .
That's why we're hiding in here . . . Shh!

Trevor Millum

Inventions to Help You Survive at School

The teacher's dodgy wig detector
The secret chocolate bar collector
The answer sheets for SATS reflector

The confiscated toy locator
The extra homework duplicator
The Literacy Hour eradicator

The dinner lady anaesthetizer
The school dinner atomizer
The fact recalling knowledge visor

The X-ray teacher's diary reader
The secret sweet in lesson feeder
The teacher's desk nest maggot breeder

Paul Cookson

Top Tip for Doing Well at School

Don't address your teacher in any of the following ways:

Boss
Mate
Dude
Kidda
Me Old China
Smelly
Horace
Bristol Rovers

And you'll do well.

Andy Seed

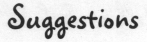

Believe yourself invisible,
Turn into a chair,
When asked an awkward question,
Remember, you're not there.

Shrink behind Jay Johnson,
Duck down to fix your shoe,
And before the weekly tables check
Leg it to the loo.

Practise writing your own notes
In inky, loopy scrawling.

Invent an infestation,
Creatures horrible and crawling.

Lose your voice for reading tests,
And if you shake with fear
Whenever asked to spell out loud,
Develop diarrhoea. (Don't try to spell it.)

Headaches, dentists, eye tests
And dead rabbits have their uses,
Just add them to your lifetime's work —
A Handbook of Excuses.

Daphne Kitching

Friends in High Places

I struggle with arithmetic
I cannot read or write
When it comes to sums or French
I am not very bright.

At PE I am hopeless
In art I cannot paint
My parents think I'm clever but
A mastermind I ain't.

In science and in ICT
I'm in the lowest set
I may be good at something but
I haven't found it yet.

So how is it at end of term
I get a good report?
Is it cos my dad's the Head?
I don't know, just a thought.

It helps to know people in high places!

Richard Caley

How to Survive Geography

Volunteer to make a map
of the school field.

Sharpen some coloured pencils
clip some paper to a board.

Off you go.

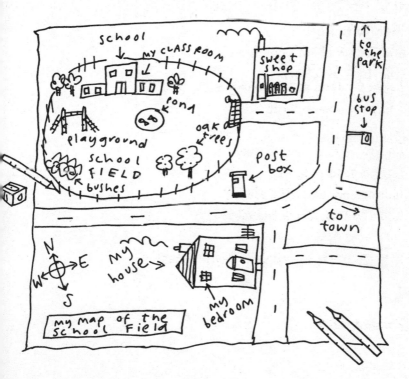

Make sure it's a very detailed map
not only of the school
but also
the school field
the roads outside the school
the sweet shop next to the school
the road to your house
the front of your house
each room in your house
especially
your bedroom.

Then go to sleep
and dream about your friends
still stuck in school.

David Harmer

Smart Ways

When teacher slips in the playground
Or when teacher falls from his chair,
Pretend you didn't see him.
Pretend that you weren't there.

If you should see your teacher
Make a silly spelling error,
Don't tell the school inspector
And fill her full of terror.

If teachers shout and scream at you
When you do something wrong,
Then, hands together, whisper prayers.
They won't stay angry long.

If teachers teach you badly,
Sit quiet, don't play the fool.
Just pack your books into your bags
And find another school!

John Kitching

A Word of Advice

Don't go near the staffroom.
That's where the teachers all tell jokes
and talk about their weekends
as they're hanging up their coats.

Keep away from the staffroom.
That's where they drink their tea
and concoct cunning plans
to upset you and me.

Don't pass by the staffroom
when the door is open wide.
A teacher's hand might reach out
and drag you inside.

And then anything could happen!

Bernard Young

Homework

It was *sitting there*, right *there* on my desk
Before, Miss, you came round:
    In a twinkling of an eye,
    In the breathing of a sigh,
    Now it's nowhere to be found!

I've really no idea how it vanished!
I wrote it last night – no, honest, honest I *did* –
    Never went out to play,
    Didn't watch *Match of the Day* . . .
    Bet you a hundred quid!

I confess I have my suspicions
(Miss, honest, I wrote *three* pages!)
   That new girl in class
   (Hair like wet grass)
   Staring at me for ages,

I've heard her mumbling funny words
I think she's jealous I have brains!
   My homework's gone
   Like snow in the sun
   Goes melted away down the drains!

Matt Simpson

How to Embarrass Teachers

Poems chosen by Paul Cookson

It's time to get even with your teachers!

Ever cringed at something your teacher has said or done? Then these poems are for you!

Now's the time to find out how a well-placed whoopee cushion (among other things) can make your teacher squirm . . .

Biting Mad

I love to make my teacher mad,
I love to make him shout
cos when his tongue gets tangled up
his new false teeth fall out!

Celia Gentles

A selected list of titles available from Macmillan Children's Books

The prices shown below are correct at the time of going to press.
However, Macmillan Publishers reserves the right to show new retail prices
on covers, which may differ from those previously advertised.

Spill the Beans

David Harmer and Paul Cookson   ISBN-13: 978-0-330-39214-3   £3.99
ISBN-10: 0-330-39214-X

How to Embarrass Teachers

David Harmer and Paul Cookson   ISBN-13: 978-0-330-44276-3   £3.99
ISBN-10: 0-330-44276-7

Silly Superstitions

Graham Denton   ISBN-13: 978-0-330-43727-5   £3.99
ISBN-10: 0-330-43727-5

Can We Have Our Ball Back, Please?

Gareth Owen   ISBN-13: 978-0-330-44048-6   £3.99
ISBN-10: 0-330-44048-9

Trick or Treat

Paul Cookson   ISBN-13: 978-0-330-42630-5   £3.99
ISBN-10: 0-330-42630-3

All Pan Macmillan titles can be ordered from our website,
www.panmacmillan.com, or from your local bookshop
and are also available by post from:

Bookpost, PO Box 29, Douglas, Isle of Man IM99 1BQ
Credit cards accepted. For details:
Telephone: 01624 677237
Fax: 01624 670923
Email: bookshop@enterprise.net
www.bookpost.co.uk

Free postage and packing in the United Kingdom